Versatility

Marian Acres

Best Wishes

Marian

Versatility

by

Marian Acres

NEW MILLENNIUM
310 Kennington Road, London SE11 4LD

Issued by New Millennium*

Printed and bound by BWD Ltd. Northolt, Middx.
.Origination by Delavi & Bailey Typesetting Bureau
ISBN 1 85845 003 9

*An imprint of The Professional Authors' & Publishers' Association

*DEDICATED TO MY MANY FRIENDS
WHO TALKED ME INTO HAVING
MY POEMS IN PRINT*

INTRODUCTION

Poetry, like lace, has woven
intricate patterns and frilled
edges.

As lace embroiders many things
to show beauty, so words are
written carefully to give such
patterns in the mind's eye.

REMINISCENCE

The day after Sunday, the day I remember
A weekly event from Jan to December
Well, Dad filled the copper and my mother the sink
With scrubbing brush and board, ne'er done in a wink.
A larger bar of green soap could be seen thro' the steam
The smell of wet washing was nobody's dream.
Came cold water rinsing and the fresh bag of "blue"
Twice through the wood mangle, the clothes were like new.
Then cold meat and pickles served with plenty of mash
Was the treat of the day for toils without cash.
Machines now take over doing "back breaking" chores
Of washing and rinsing and cleaning the floors
Yet, I won't forget how we turned out in splendour
the day after Sunday, --- the day I remember.

FRIDAY.

The coalman heaved a ton into the cellar
Left, folding sacks and coughing on the dust
For Friday nights, as far as I remember
We had the fires all laid and lit by dusk.

The metal bath placed neatly by the tiled hearth
Filled from scullery copper, standing there
How we enjoyed the friendly fire with our bath
Then, in night clothes clean, to climb the stair.

Central Heating, bathroom, now a pleasure
To have a shower which we love so well
But the memories I will always treasure
Soap and soda replaced by shower gel.

THE POND

Oh! look, --- just by that reed
I think you'll find indeed
Our friends have truly made a pond
No! --- not towards the shed
Just by the flower bed
Don't raise your eyes to look beyond.

Well, mind the rockery
I'm surprised you can't see
The waterfall and the lily
Yes. I'm sad to relate
You're getting in a state
And I'm feeling --- rather silly.

So, how about that frog
The grass, the fish, the bog ---
Perhaps we shouldn't stay too long
Your sight is really poor
Mind the steps! --- yes --- one more
Whoops a buttercup --- crash --- splash --- gone!

LIFE

Life, you have a changing face
We start with dimple put in place
We grow and grow into our clothes
Need bigger hankies for our nose
Youthful figures we try to keep
Alas, --- we lose them while we sleep
As we learn what it's all about
Becoming portly or even stout
Worse is to come, and all too soon
We end up wrinkled --- like a prune.

FOUR WATCHING EYES

A sparrow was feeding, it's baby
An amusing sight to see
The poor little mite was a dreadful sight
Bedraggled, and wet as could be.

He tottered about unsteadily
Beneath mother's protecting wing
His legs were weak, and with open beak
He chirped and tried to sing.

I knew he was very hungry
He was taking food galore
Ate every grain, with mouth wide again
He started calling for more.

I wasn't the only one watching
A cat found it interesting too
But mother so wise did realise
and, --- away the two sparrows flew.

SPRING

Away from London's busy thoroughfare
In April of the year
I travel to meet the sweet country air
Knowing that Spring is here.

To feel the cool breeze caressing my face
And ruffling through my hair
Helping to convey the spiritual grace
Of Nature's kindly care.

See flowers nodding with delightfulness
Dancing to spring's first call
Stately trees in new finery and dress
Looking down on all.

This is when I'm content and feel at ease
Away from London's roar
And of all the season's memories
It's Spring - that I adore.

ERE THEY RETURN

In dingy homes with ears alert
Patiently they watch and wait
Hearts that pine to see the men home
Because the boat is late
Though the weather is bad and the're away
The fishermen are not afraid
They brave the storms to do their job
And come to Britain's aid.

When the raging seas send billowing waves
Dashing wildly against the rocks
And screaming seagulls swoop the air
Flying out to sea in flocks
Then folk know the boat's returning
With shimmering catch aboard
And above the sea's terrific call
Prayers --- ascending to the Lord.

CHRISTMAS

A kind thought at Christmas
Wrapped with sweetest feeling
Bound with the strength of friendship
Tied with a knot of love
Given straight from the heart
Offered with outstretched hand
Be it ever so humble
Will receive the warmest welcome.

WINTER

When night brings crispness to the air
And you can feel it everywhere
When flowers droop and fallen leaves
Strew the ground beneath the trees.
Just take a look into the night
And see frost forming - glistening - white.

When morning comes there's once again
Frost patterning the window pane
A strange design of ferns and leaves
The wondrous touch, which man agrees
Perfection, to artistic eyes.
Then Winter's here - to realise.

A SMILE

You pause and think
Just for a while
How good to see
A cheerful smile
To feel it's warmth
to see it's grace
Such improvement
To any face.

I stopped and thought
Just as I said
I did a grin
My heart was lead
From the mirror
A welcome sight
A smile came back
It proves I'm right.

A TROUBLED MIND

How often do we find
When in a troubled mind
That we'd like to hit our head against a wall.

How often do we feel
That it simply can't be real
And we'll wake up soon and find we've dreamt it all.

Life is that way you know
The years will come and go
And skies above just change from blue to grey.

But if we persevere
Our head will slowly clear
And send the dark clouds rolling on their way.

A SECOND THOUGHT

When the day turns out a failure
I try to put it right
I work hard at my job all day
And forget troubles over night.
But, when next morning I awake
My first thought is often - Oh!
I didn't do that certain thing
Or ring up - "So and So".
Well, then I start off once again
With this thought of my mind
To greet the new day with a smile
But, like many others, find
The smile's reduced to drooping lip
When even "work" to put away
Is once more there before my eyes
The same as yesterday.

DREAM

It stood on a hill
I think of it still
Eyes winking in the sun
Behind, were tall trees
And a stream to please
O'er stones and rocks did run.

White painted gutters
Matching the shutters opened to meet the air
The windows were lead
Chintz curtains pale red
A cat was curled up there.

An arch with a rose
Flowers fit for shows
Lovingly grew so bold
Landscaped and lawned
Picturesque --- adorned
With a board standing --- marked "sold".

HER ROYAL HANDBAG

"H.R.H." in stately dress
The name we give the Queen
With every fashioned outfit
A handbag can be seen.

What really could be in them?
For money she'll not need
No cheque book, and no purse
To fill the space indeed.

The Key - to let herself in?
Someone's always home
Still the handbag hangs there
All by itself alone.

Could it hold a credit card?
I doubt if that is so
She's never seen to "make-up"
So that's another - "no"

Well, a handbag's always full
All but the "kitchen sink"
What she has put inside
It truly makes me think.

I know it holds her glasses
For they're to read a speech
Identification card?
Perhaps a handkerchief?

We never see it opened
No "ins and outs" I stress
Not like mine I am sure
Always in a mess.

A card which says "I am Queen"
Perhaps is there inside
"If lost, please return me -
Buck Palace - I reside."

"TIPS"

A menial job is better by far
Than no job at all - whoever you are
For after all - somebody has to make the tea!

What, for us, does the future have in store
Perhaps, just a living and not much more
Well, After all - somebody has to make the tea!

No land of plenty for sometime to come
A job would be of value for everyone
For after all - somebody has to make the tea!

All housewives suffer "the great indoors"
Cooking, cleaning and all menial chores
Well, after all - somebody has to make the tea!

JOURNEY

I saw poppies nodding in a field of grain
As if they were talking about the rain
And the rabbits playing, their white tails showing
Amid the sun's rays, so slowly going,
The trees shaking sadly, as I passed them by
With horses beneath them, just to keep dry
Farms and thatched cottages, loomed into my view
But, when deeply looking, they had gone too
The windows of houses sparkling with raindrops
Have curtains snugly drawn as the light stops
Then the winking lights of the town come again
As I reflect the journey home - by train.

TALL TREE

Tall tree, I see you from my room, from my chair
Tall tree, I wake each day, Knowing you'll be there
Grown free, you're there in your finery and dress
Grown free, you're display is perfect I confess
Could be, you landmark jets as to base they fly
Could be, you protect our roof as you're so high
Tall tree, against all skies your beauty divine
Tall tree, Truly a master piece of design
For me, it is a carpenter's little joke
For me, There's truthfully nothing quite like oak!
Oh magnificent tall tree

THE PENDULUM

The best of us will <u>find</u> it
For things we want to do
We hurry not to <u>lose</u> it
From every point of view.

How often we just <u>make</u> it
So we have some to <u>spare</u>
To give to other people
We show how much we care.

If we are apt to <u>take</u> it
We make it up again
They say it costs us money
So we should not complain.

We keep it and we <u>beat</u> it
And tap it with our feet
Then we try to <u>kill</u> it
Our schedule to complete.

But it still creeps up on us
Of this I have no doubt
Treat "Time" with all respects folks
For <u>"Time"</u> will soon run out!

INTO THE NIGHT

The swirling wind took the rain in glistening sheets
        along the street
A whirl of waste paper followed its tracks, ending
        in the gutter
Outside the darkened shops the street signs swung
        and rattled, stretched to meet
Failing in all their efforts excepting moanful
        squeaks to utter.

No soul strod the blackened town, no footsteps
        heard above the wind and rain
I stood in the doorway looking intrepidly
        into the night
Wondering why I had made such a hazardous
        journey again
My coat collar up I turned directly, remaining
        out of sight.

A dim light glinted a welcome ray through
        the velvet curtain
Above the gale, a dog howled, I shivered and
        yet I could not stay
Knowing that in spite of all things, it was over
        I was certain
A clattering dustbin lid, I started the car
        and drove away.

AWAY FROM TOWN

I've watched the rolling banks of billowy clouds
            that sweep across the Dorset sky
And seen endless trees give unmatched patterns
            to open landscapes,
Rising from the clouds, giving edging to all
            the panoramic views.
I've seen the heron leap the roof tops,
            the fish ponds to espy.

The pretty gardens of every hue, the thatched
            cottages standing proudly by
The winding lanes and open plains I've travelled
            enjoying scenes
Of sheep and cows and horses that I had not
            had the pleasure of seeing before
I've seen the heron leap the rooftops, the
            fish ponds to espy.

The beauty of the countryside, the pleasure of
            the country towns, the sea and I
Will merge to form a film of silent colour
            like morning mist
No rain on my parade now that I have
        made my choice of space to spread around me
I've seen the heron leap the rooftops, the
            fish ponds to espy.

WICKER CHAIR

Old wicker chair, old wicker chair
You creak and squeak though nobody's there
With back so straight and arms so strong
You look so great, to me you belong.

I sit in you, you have a moan
Even though I've a cushion of foam
You join in with the talking point
I think you creak from every joint.

Old wicker chair, old wicker chair
You make this noise to show that you're there
Make not a sound, should I take sleep
Or back you go to the old scrap heap!

TOMORROW

Tomorrow comes a little quicker
As it gets a little bolder
For it very soon becomes <u>today</u>.

Catching up then, even slicker
Making us feel a little older
Fleeting to become yesterday.

Pages of time how forthcoming
Always telling, always turning
No allowances to mark the place.

Like the sound of distant drumming
Striving to keep life's bright fire burning
So that there's <u>tomorrow</u> to face.

BOURNEMOUTH

> Bournemouth
> In
> Is
> want
> You
> Everything
> But it's always up a hill
> Not for disabled or O.A.Ps.
> It can make me feel quite ill
> Bournemouth
> In
> Is
> Want
> You
> Everything
> But I prefer "on the flat"
> I'll take what I get in Poole High Street
> Have breath to spare -- and that's that!

LULLABY

Smiling eyes
Gaze at me
For a while
To make my day
Dimpled cheeks
Heavenly
When you look
At me that way

Fingers small
Tightly hold
Onto me
A bond we Know

Dream a while
Pleasantly
As you sleep
So you will grow

Near my heart
Can't you see
You're the one
That I adore

Cradle you
Lovingly
In my arms
For evermore

POEMS

You know I try to write them
The fire in you to kindle
The rhythm and the subject
Your interest must not dwindle
Perhaps a little tiring
But no doubt it could be worse
Perhaps you'd like it better
If I only wrote one verse!

A FISHY TALE

On a cold slab
Wet or dried
Laid in rows
Side by side
Fully displayed
The fisherman's pride
Your Friday meal
Baked or fried
Grilled or steamed
With sauce denied
Poached or boiled
With sauce applied
It's much the same
Which ever way tried
The taste you'll acquire
Then you'll decide
It really is good
You're satisfied.

COLD COMFORT

Watery eyes
And runny nose
Heaps of hankies
Terrific blows
A graveyard cough
And aching head
Just think of work
And feel half dead.
Leave of absence
To be explained
Because we're tired
And feeling drained.
It could be worse
So we are told.
Oh - how wretched
The common cold!

SLUGS

We have a reluctant hedgehog
Who comes most every night
To feed on the slugs and snails
But he can't get it right

Maybe he should throw a party
Bring his friends for a feast
To help keep the garden balance
Beans --- we've lost half at least

Don't want to revert to slug pellets
They're not a welcome sight
Perhaps when he comes tomorrow
He'll have an appetite!

A FRIEND

We find them in the car park
Taking up our parking space
Abandoned on grass verges
This is most common place

Lying on their side in streams
So enhancing Nature's view
Seen also in back gardens
For flowers of different hue

From harbours and deep rivers
They are dragged upon the scene
The breeding season happens
And there's two where one has been

Could really do without this
Hide and seek so jolly
Who discards a friend indeed?
The supermarket trolley

THE BATH

Four were taking a bath
On that find day in June
Yet there could have been five
But there was no more room.

Water was everywhere
They jumped and splashed about
As more tried to get in
They pushed each other out.

I could have joined in too
As I was feeling hot
But I daren't move at all
Such enjoyment would stop.

They dried off in the sun
To watch them made me laugh
So enriched the pleasure
Of a garden bird bath.

HOME GROAN!

Up the garden path
Just behind the Shed
The tortoise hides there
I can see his head

Winter, and he's inside
In a box of straw
And in the Spring Time
He makes for the door

On to the veg patch
For salads, his joy
Having slept for months
He's a hungry boy

A surprise in store
The view so estranged
He's to search because
The garden we've changed.

PATTERNS

Warily picking my way across the tiled floor
Leaving muddy footprints for all to see
Prominently showing on the lighter colours,
I thought of "Macavity".
Perhaps the new blemishes would not be noticed
Mixed with the other marks or, would
Fade with passing hours.
It was raining cats and dogs outside,
Pardon the expression.
I took a quick drink and decided on a nap
After washing, to remove the day.
I would wait until I heard footsteps.
What of It! After all,
I had used the flap.

TOWN GARDEN

I am walking past your garden
Often I walk past
Railings close to door
Glancing to see green shoots
Ah! But it's winter when all about lies still.

I don't hurry past your garden
Or yet scurry past
Pleasure through railings,
Seeing coloured array
Ah! A summer display from your window sill.

MIRRORS

Line each day with brightness
and the mirrored reflection
shall be of diamonds
though round your neck may hang
the cheapest beads.

A smile will be of pearls
such glistening whiteness
Glimpse eyes of sapphires
with lips of red rubies
without blemish.

To behold the beauty
look deeply to imagine
these jewels of desire
or round your neck may hang
the cheapest beads.

ALONE

As evening dons it's grey velvet cloak
Across a deepened glowing sky of varied red
And the blackbird close by, tells repeatedly
The colour is pink, pink, pink; the hedgehog comes.

I hear the scraping of his bristles
As he crawls beneath the side gate
He walks with a four legged limpness
To nibble a slither of lardy cake crumpled by the
                                    backdoor.
I listen to his lip smacking, over this delicacy
He is oblivious to my eyes pursuing such enjoyment
Then, with avid interest,, I see him trot the garden
Nosing the plants and hiding 'neath drooping leaves.

Every night he comes, almost at the same time,
The activities of home, to him, are no threat
I watch, until the failing light holds my view
I am a lonely watcher of a lone hedgehog run.

FROM THE SHORE

The sea stretched to the horizon like a
     greyish carpet
Shades of light and darker patches as fluffy
     clouds hid the sun

The waves sparkled in places when the sun beamed
     its rays upon them
I saw then, little white horses.

The roar and the turn of each wave broke
     the silent tranquillity of my thoughts
Various coloured pebbles shuffled about
     uneasily on the shore.
Waves hissed as they rippled through them
     and then drawing back to the sea
I saw then, little white horses.

I felt pebbles edging my toes as I
     stood feeling each wave
It was good to hear, feel and
     look upon the sea
Realising all the time of the power
     the vastness and the strength
I saw then, little white horses.

IT'S A BARGAIN

Enjoyment in the market towns of Britain
A feeling of friendship everywhere
The stalls of canvas topping welcomes shoppers
Above which cries of "Fifty pence a pair".

The crowds gather around to get a bargain
What e'er the weather they'll be there
And above the bags laden with shopping
Came the call of "Fifty pence a pair".

The chip and burger stall for hungry hunters
It's a jungle of people I declare
On reaching home I had socks for Christmas
Yes, and all for fifty pence a pair.

WAITING

She sat by the window, peering into
the street from behind the net curtain.
Memories she had many, the chance
to tell of them but few.
The milkman walked the path and left
the usual pint and walked the path
again, with the chinking of bottles.
When, as a girl she had collected the milk
in a jug, then, there was .time for a friendly chat.
She stroked the cat, who would listen to
her every word, whilst rubbing against
her wrinkled hand.
She straightened the curtain.
Maybe there will be a letter tomorrow.

HAPPY BIRTHDAY

As the last log burning on the fire drops
and the poker rakes the ashes through
with a final tap sounding on the hearth.

As the candle flames dance on the cake
and the wax melts and lodges on the side
before a breath is heard to blow them out.

As the balloons outside lose their roundness
and the last child gives the final click to the door,
So I view the devastation, to be tackled tomorrow.

NO ESCAPE

Like the moving water of the stream
glistening as it gushes over the rocks
disappearing into stillness where the waiting
pike lies.

Like the howling wind in the woods
as it races through the trees, in escaping
to the hills, where the perimeter
fence lies.

Like feelings of youthfulness,
a rainbow, which eventually comes
down to earth, so hiding the fountain
of Youth where "The secret of
Youth" lies.

LIKEN TO VELVET

Little heads were raised, nodding their
approval to the gentle breeze.
Little faces, of blue yellow and blushed
red, bestowed the velvet touch and grace.
Ne'er tall, yet understanding in
unsurpassable beauty as they
Faced the world.
Would that I could always smile
like the Pansy.

ESCAPISM

A summer house is a corner of paradise
A quiet place of retreat, providing
a different perspective to the garden.
A place where the world goes around
without notice and where dreams and future plans flour-
ish.
Flowers are viewed in magnificent
colour and glory, some for the
picking, and some to seed for next
year's growth.
Lost in a space for decisions made
over afternoon tea, it is then
widely noticed, after all reminiscing
that the lawn needs cutting again.

MEMORY FILE

"Why can't you remember things Grandad?
The question I'm sure you know
You've closed your eyes, are you asleep?
Tell me , when will I grow?

"Im sorry I dozed young fellow,
But you see I'm much older than you,
I've such a lot in my Memory File
It takes longer to sort it through."

"You'll grow like the plants in the garden
You'll stand up straight and tall
And when you grow up, you'll understand
Why it takes time, to remember it all."

WHAT AM I ?

What is specifically ME?
When my organs will work in another
Have I lost my identity ?
What is ME, I have yet to discover.

RECESSION

The factory floor is empty now
Where I worked with Bill and Joe
The machines are standing silent
Just as if they really know
Their stiffening joints have rusted
And no longer will they go.

The dust and rubble everywhere
The tools which were left behind
The memories that I treasure
Return instantly to mind
Through broken glass I viewed the scene
Of government so unkind.

Without work now are all we three
So we join the millions throng
from closures and redundancies
A world where we don't belong.
We wait for Britain's future role
From a country that went wrong.

MORE TO LIFE THAN "DUST"?

We have over fished the sea
And over crowed the roads
And we're over crowding the earth

We are polluting the air
For future folk to live
We should value life - for its worth

We litter all the streets
Though we're proud of being "green"
To say this now, I must

There won't be "more to life"
If we don't "shape up" I fear
And clean up never ending "dust".

1914 - 1918   1939 - 1945
TO OUR FIGHTING MEN

'Twas not for the sake of a medal
Nor for the sake of winning a name
Never to be placed in the limelight
For the sake of achieving fame

'Twas because they knew of their duty
And knew the job had to be done
For many a man had fought and fell
Before a victory was won.

'Twas a long, long, job that they suffered
So a kind thought for all who enlisted.
For men like these did England credit ---
Without them --- would we have existed?

HEAT FIRE AND ICE

Goodbye the Yugoslavia I remember.
Hvar, Island of lavender heather and honey
Tiny churches and markets in the sun.
Kranska Gora, with high ranging snow capped
peaks into the sky.
Chair lifts to top thrusting deep into
the frozen atmosphere.
Hotels, neatly placed nestling in the
valleys, commanding panoramic
views of all around.
Cultivated land surrounding pretty
cottages having balconies dressed
with vegetables, drying in sunlight
for storage.
Is it the same now?
Mostar, and the prayers which were chanted in the
mosque
The shoes left outside and the feet that were washed.
River of ice blue shimmering in the heat
The marble bridge that was hosed to repel the heat
so that we could cross.
The open fronted shanty shops, selling
Leather brass and copper.
Nerium trees in drooping heavy flower
perfuming the air,
Air which was hot and humid.
Swallow and Krk Falls, deep and deeper yet,
The rushing waters and the cold in the depth.
Now, the cold in my heart.